SOCIAL MEDIA

SOCIAL MEDIA

MARY MACPHERSON

THE CUBA
PRESS

For Peter

Cover and author photographs by Peter Black.
Cover and book design by Paul Stewart.
Edited by Madison Hamill and Mary McCallum.

A catalogue record for this book is available from the
National Library of New Zealand.
ISBN 978-1-98-859504-7

Printed in Aotearoa New Zealand by
Wakefields Digital, Wellington.

The Cuba Press
Box 9321, Wellington 6141
Aotearoa New Zealand

Contents

ONE

Smoke 9
Palaces 10
Inventing a person 11
New Zealand holiday 12
EFTPOS dance 13
Ode to motels 14
Litter 15
Dog mask 17
Exit 19
Dog 20

TWO

Charge 23
River 24
Y as X 25
Name game 26
Taboo 27
Subtraction 28
One life 30
R channels David Attenborough 31
S imagines R 32
Threads 33
Bam 35
Foreign languages 36

S wakes up 37
Gifts 39
Reconstructions 40

THREE

On being unwilling to click
'I forgot my password' 43
A short history of sightseeing 44
Instructed to write a poem called Home 45
Spring story 46
Touch phone 47
The silences 48
At Moeraki 50
Bees 53
Fall of the leaf 55

Notes 59
Acknowledgements 60

ONE

Smoke

Music from behind the hedge
rises wild over sharp leaves

saying, dance like a tree.
You imagine a leaking

leaning sofa crashing
the party: the big guest

everyone climbs on. O yes,
you love the imagined other.

You pace the porch, loving and hating.
Smoke rises from remote fires.

Next morning, birdcalls
spiral in cool air; something's gone

out of sight, something's
flickering in its place.

Palaces

When it became warmer, we mooned over flowers,
lit again among hunks of grass. We found marbles
behind the dresser and remembered palaces
in the swirls of colour. Shops meant something too.
We loved the fierce desire for things and our beautiful
imaginary selves. Almost overnight, the sad-faced dairy
became a darkened window with a spot-lit bath,
then leapt to its future as a dog grooming establishment.
We thought of the summers when buying three pairs of togs
was as normal as sand. Silver gates guarded our wishes.
They were forever before us – lights down a suburban street,
the dark flesh of leaves, petals like dancers in a sodium night.

Inventing a person

First, they'll need your house,
its bricks burning radium-red. The mother
with cool dry hands and a particular hallway
with doors opening to shadowed rooms.
You must give them urgent teenage desires:
kissing, sex, a horse, an opposite life.
Then they need a friend – plump, ginger-haired
with freckles – to remember later
with shame or tenderness. When the friend speaks
of holidays, boys or stones, you must know the light
that goes on or the stain that darkens the mind,
and what gets reflected in tall windows.
Then you must give the friend opinions about apples,
walking home in the dark, their friend's habit
of chewing their hair, and know whether your person
notices the friend noticing the chewing.

New Zealand holiday

The weather blew through us. Wind
and rain driving through bones as we strained
to pull the cart of belief. The forest
was dirty, sullen. You looked for the slash
of a road sign to reel us in. I believed
in a beach that stretched further than thought
but held fast as water flew from our wheels.
We spoke as if speaking would rope us
to our intentions – intended more by me
but negotiated silently between us
like sniffing animals. I thought of being told
New Zealand photography was more about place,
Australian, more ephemeral. It was like
seeing myself as a child hot and blinking
in front of a hedge. Moments
on either side falling like sheer cliffs.
Was that still me, in spite of the journeys
and grown-up body? When the car rocked,
our hearts skipped, being there with toetoe,
a gravel-edged ditch, shrouded mānuka.

EFTPOS dance

'Would you buy a car called *Dingo Pop*?' he asked.
She did a little character dance in her strong black shoes
raising a snowstorm of receipts. Ben M checked out their groceries.
Krishna 15 drove them to the city, but Kamal 5 substituted
to take them home. Daniel sold them T-shirts, but as she entered
her PIN on flaccid keys, her stomach tightened. She detested
aged EFTPOS – she was afraid her money would vanish
down the spiral cord. The whole glittery aisle did a T-shirt dance.
But Toni Perfect replied to her nervous query within
the required time and signed – *Kind regards*. It made her feel
faintly loved, then pitied, by a stranger.

Ode to motels

Motel, motel – here's to you with your sliding
door and fumbly key we always try upside down.
Your regulation room, barely-lit room, refurbished
room, your bed taking up all the room. Motel
we see giant flowers on the cover pulled so tight,
the close-lipped daisies cover, the matching-the-curtains
cover, your cool sheets and rock mattress – wide
as a boat – that we've rented, together with your contents,
for the night. There's the stumpy bench for our rustling food
bags and crumbs, the dwarf fridge with its ice-cube icebox,
little milk carton (regular or trim?) and implements – knives –
two (one blunt), grater, toaster, fry pan etc, but never a garlic
press. Motel, we sit on your upright, firm, sagging, velour,
over-cushioned sofa to watch the news in stretched images
aided by your spongy remote. We panicked at the No
Vacancy signs and you let us in for your special rate,
going rate, heart-stopping motel-with-a-view rate. Now we have
thin soaps to pop out of flowered packets, round upmarket
ones to claw out of tissue, a springy shower cubicle, and heavy
heavy towels in spanking white or older green. We know
we could be sleeping in the car, or snarling and desperate,
driving at 10pm, so we had to upgrade to your new chain
rate, where we got a bigger bathroom shelf, smart toilet-roll
holder, skinny closet, a clear view, belle view – mountains plus
water – and a glimpse of the neighbour's pool table inside
their garage.

Litter

Have you ever used the spare buttons
that come with clothes? Do you save
the safety pins from dry cleaning?
Have you ever used them to hold
your trousers together? Did you use –
a stout chrome pin or dainty gold?
Which would you rescue
the family pet or your computer?
Do you think your computer is upset
when it gurgles or whirrs?
In foreign cities, how many knobs or handles
have you turned the wrong way?
Do you believe you can do anything?
How do you feel when someone imitates you –
annoyed or flattered? Do you feel guilty
when you imitate someone else?
Could you recite all your usernames
and passwords? Have you ever thought
of them as litter? How often do you choose
the name of your first family pet
as a security question? Will you vanish
if you can't remember your PIN? Could you
describe a colour without reference
to other colours? Do you panic when faced
with unfamiliar taps? How do you react to cords
that have lost their appliances?

Have you ever tossed an orphaned cord?
How do you deal with devices
with missing manuals? Should you know
everything? Are you afraid
of what's underground? How do you feel
when old bottles surface in a garden?
Old rubber balls?

Dog mask

Our red tongues lick the electronics. We love the outdoors
and bounding about with names on our collar – look that's us
wearing Fair Isle in the sunny mountains. Our marks are found
behind desks and pot plants, blending discreetly with the walls.
Am I silly or convincing?
Lately, I've wondered what it means to give a room a name.
Is it like naming your dog?
Once, I found a mountain in a hotel corridor with flimsy yet
claustrophobic walls. There was also an important sea
and legendary explorers whose exploits I had to google.
Am I being superficial?
When I asked about the mountain, the sea and the explorers
spoons clattered and my ancient computer dribbled answers
down its front. Husky and Doberman were ready to haul the mess
of my thinking to a room where ankles can be seen at the bottom
of frosted glass. I wanted to put a dog mask on and bound through

the office at night, leaping the reception desk, weaving through the open plan. Secure doors would fly open at my approach. Outside, city lights would spin in the growling night.

Exit

Caught in a strangely angled room with unusual walls,
I forget the way to the scene where cars go by like shadows

and Marilyn blows her kiss. Oh, I've got digital pāua gloves
for picking through silence, but in the street of pollinated spas

I don't know what to want. The signs call out – *A Pleasant Place*
to Stay. We're not as expensive as we look! Genuine mineral pools.

Genuine private mineral pools! The man opposite has moons
in his eyes – so far away he's like a plant that's drawn its life

back inside. My desire is in a trolley nuzzling a car-park tree.
If I could remember my life, I'd find a glittering street – heat rising,

shadows under deep verandahs. Lost in the procession of cars
and people, I'd never know if I'd turned the wrong way.

Dog

She thought of herself as a portrait.
Not the kind she was afraid of
as a child, with expressions
sharp as arrows. In her picture
fingers rippled across
the rough heartbeat of a fence.
When she looked through
her curtain of hair, lips a soft O,
people and trees appeared
as a faded transparency. Her sense of not
belonging was a devoted ragged dog
snuffling alongside. Except she forgot
to imagine a leash so the dog figured
it was free to run to the glittering bush
at the end of the street. Alone, she practised
stepping outside the frame. Saying *really*
and answering quiz questions
and grinning. Sometimes she got it
and buildings moved out
of the shadows, revealing
themselves solid as fences.
It was a fine day and the world
stood up for her. Shadows lay down
at her feet.

TWO

Charge

Write a poem about battery anxiety, says X. There's a list of stuff
he wants poems about – hard, bright ideas – but mostly Y forgets
to write the ideas down. Now she's writing a silver iPad poem, also
incorporating a snug plastic-encased Android phone, a bristling
electric shaver, another phone, several nuggety camera batteries,
plus cords. What will the poem look like? Suck suck – electricity.
Can I call when I've left the snaking power at home? R is busy
writing about scarce rare earth minerals. S goes backwards
and unplugs everything. X tells him it's bad for the batteries.
Y says this is S being S – what she's after is the mad rush to get
everything charged for night and day and having that pulsing
in your brain – except, she can't imagine caring enough.
She twitches about what it costs, and what would happen
if some devices went on holiday? (Could she persuade X
to charge the iPad every second day?) X says the poem has gone
off the rails. He wants silver devotion and panic about tangled
chargers, dark at the bottom of the suitcase (what goes with what?)
and supposing you left the phone charger behind and couldn't call,
even if you were angry.

River

R worries about the plants. The summer they've had, and lately,
the rain that's poured from the sky. In his worry – a moment's darkness
in his eyes – there are gardens of stressed ferns and dahlias, stricken
with incurable diseases. X worries about his small shiny dog, finding
his fears in dreams where the dog is slippery or broken so he can't
hold her above people's heads on the crowded train. Y worries about
what X worries about. He should worry about more meaningful things –
perhaps the dog is an avatar for these fears? She puts her worry
into the river of things she cures in her mind. S worries about the sales
of his inventions, ideas that have followed him for years – all this
may not be redeemed. X and Y talk about S's worry, turning it over
and over. Y worries that they're being smug. She knows how desire
blots out the sun. She writes the word 'replaceable' in a notebook
and worries about slipperiness. S dwells on the thought of having
no plants to eat – he'd leave immediately for another country. He invites
X and Y to go with him. His friends are quiet, worrying about how
they'd earn a living, and how they couldn't live exactly as they do now.

Y as X

When Y writes as X she thinks she should write sentences like jabs in a boxing match, but pulled at the last minute by a sudden funniness. How does he do that? She looks at X's writing and sees his sentences are often shockingly short. X would never write a word like 'disbenefit', then in a long parenthesis explain that, surprisingly, the word does exist and how he feels embarrassed he didn't know, and that the person who used the word had a blocky confidence they would rise in the organisation,
so took words from the course rather than older ones with their shabby disadvantages and how this upsets X in ways he can't explain. Close parenthesis.

When X sees Y's attempts to write as him, he's startled by the bluntness of the text. He's become an alarmingly savage person. Put in 'please' there and there, he tells Y. And thank her. End by thanking her.

Name game

X believes he lives inside the TV and Y
is going to turn him off
calls for lemons when he means limes
says 'you know those dogs', meaning
anything he wants to talk about
names his car Mad Mouse
his bike The Fast Knife
approves of Mandarin meaning Mondrian
claps for Dvořák when Djokovic wins a set
calls S 'wet dog', R 'the parakeet'
himself 'the slimy rat' baring
his tobacco teeth in a furious grin
his shiny dog, Willy the kid
or any mellifluous name
belonging to a foreign cricketer
says his new business associate is bushy-eyed
and brightly-tailed, exploding the room with giggles
writes that he wants a conservation
with her – Y reassembles the letters
so the meaning folds tidily – tiddly
says X dancing in his underpants threatening
to go to the conservation like that
looking to Y to spank him
except Y is gazing out the window
at inland gulls thinking how serene
the harsh birds look soaring across rooves
like any fear made pleasing by distance

Taboo

Y worries a lot about snipping off the satin straps
that keep slipping out of her T-shirt. She's okay
with baby-blue and buttons across one shoulder,
but then she finds tongues across her neck; dirty words.
There's the taboo of new and, if she cuts, one day she'll peer
into a motel wardrobe where the clothes rail is too high
and an ironing board takes up half the space. With no straps
and only two difficult thief-proof hangers, she'll – fuck –
poverty/war/oppression/clothingsweatshops/icemelting/
endoftheplanet/cutstraps.

Subtraction

1.

How can a person be imagined? Y wonders. She's inside a story
about two people who write to each other for years.
When they meet, the peeking blinds and thick lace tablecloth
fly up and cover their heads. Descriptions slip like unstable earth.

2.

What would she say about S? Kindness shot through with envy?
No – more like extravagantly open.[1] Something about reeling
the world backwards, until an order that matters to S
is revealed.[2]

3.

You think I'm just a figment of your brain, X says to Y. (Y isn't sure
that figment is the right word.)

You think you can just make up things about me.

If you turn off that part of your brain, I'll disappear.

Y reaches for X's soft leather jacket which smells (intoxicatingly) of wounded pride.

She wants to see herself entwined – a word that belongs
in one of those old songs her parents used to sing in the car.

How would X look without her?

How would he live without her disapproval?

Would she be a duller person without his clever little dog?

1. Y has learned this technique from the many interviews she's been to. 'What would ( ) say about you?' She plunges into the milky lake of words. Quick clear beats to the nearest raft. 'Get there, get there,' is what she thinks.

2. Would it be more accurate if she described herself and compared S with that description? Can she only say who a person is, by subtracting them from another?

One life

In his tree house R is reading a book that suggests a more hopeful time is cracking open. There are titles like, *How men and women have slowly learned to have more interesting conversations; How humans have repeatedly lost hope, and how new encounters, and a new pair of spectacles revive them* – and section dividers – *Three new kinds of emotional adhesive* & *Does punctuality bring happiness?* From below comes the chuckle-chain of hens. Birdcalls fill the air like pines before the wind. A slow smile spreads across R's face as he thinks of Theo over 20 years ago surveying history, one life at a time. His own resistance germinated from his study of lessons from the past applied to misshapen events in his friends' lives. R rocks on his cloud porch, safe from polyester meringues in the world below. How he'd like to haul his friends up past their knobbly fears – *How even astrologers resist their own destiny* – so his thoughts can open and scatter as seeds of pinecones.

R channels David Attenborough

How is it for the worm? R closes
his eyes to darkness and raw
warm earth. There's stabbing, a blaze
of steel (do worms comprehend steel?)
earth crumbling, tunnels collapsing,
squirming, clods and rain. Pink
succulence is exposed and air slips
through skin.

(R now understands that by gouging
a tangled mass of roots from the soil
he has destroyed cities.)

A sleek bird-boat touches down.
Beady-eyed, the thrush darts forward
across fresh earth – *Oh* – half the worm
is bobbed back, then the pincer
flashes again.

R needs to share his dismay. Y, even X, would do.
How should he illuminate the sequence?
He needs the bird's point of view – something
about needy young beaks. He needs the worm's
point of view. Himself as Man. The raw earth.
Prey.

S imagines R

S wonders how R can look down a path
and see a cathedral in the trees. What looked
like shitty branches, arch over the gravel
and it's pleasant that birds visit often
with the seeds of even more trees.
But would R play endlessly with his cat?
Spend a morning bowling overs
to his nephews? S reaches for R
but can only imagine a cat's wet fur.
Anyway, he prefers the rectangles he's dug
in the lawn, and the carrots he's planted
in memory of his mother and her narrow waist.

Threads

R sees things sprouting in the plain bus-stop world and wants to trace
the threads that lead all over the place.

His list includes the brittle sunburnt grass surrounding the coloured-by-
crayons shelter.

How many times have the seeds been down to the earth
and back up again?

R doesn't care if the big yellow buses slow down and drivers look at him
to see if he's going to get on.

He's listening to tiny shrieks from the Playcentre.

His job is to remember its former life as a Closed Brethren church
with walls up past its ears.

He suspects, further back, there've been other uses for the land –
a contested rectangle with leftover bush?

S finds him – 'C'mon man, it's freezing' – but R is considering black wires
stretching from shafts of concrete to every home.

Inside the lighted houses are people with enormous lives.

S says he's moved by weatherboards and fences – generations of hands
caring for families.

He sits beside R in the shelter and starts to cry.

Y thinks it's peculiar and dangerous to live at the bus stop.

Perhaps R could take photographs and think about
what everything means, at home.

X tells her that R is a foolish artist but the bus stop world is his vision.

Y feels confused and anxious.

She tells her friends that she knows this artist who lives at the bus stop – rather cool, actually.

R talks to reporters who demand to know what he's doing in the shelter.

He's towing the world towards stop 4261.

S talks to passers-by. He believes he's kind and good with people.

'You have to make them come home,' Y says to X.

She wrings her hands as if she's squeezing out her anxious heart.

'Bugger off,' says X who's searching for his wandering dog.

He stands at the back door, calling and calling.

Bam

I sat near a tall woman who loved netball, but had crashed
and hurt her back, S tells his new friend. (Tired of her sly doubts,
he's stopped telling Y about ideas for films, preferring the excitement
of a new confessor.) For weeks, the woman couldn't train or pick up
her baby, but sat straight all day taking calls from people confused
about how to register, or why they had to pay, or yelling
about the government. Her voice, still calm, became firmer as she said
the same thing in different ways, like she was searching for the moment
to snatch the ball and blaze down the court, yellow hair flying,
to her physio. What if I filmed hundreds of women like her, said S,
or five at least, the days of explaining then letting off steam
or catching the supervisor's eye and moving quickly to the next –
and the callers who'd maybe banged the phone down, then said
'bitch' or 'cunt', going on to water the plants or walk the dog,
jerking the lead when the dog stopped to sniff – and what the women
did after work, going hard at roller derby or rushing to pick up
the baby so they could get dinner on. The film would be about
when the women and callers collided then sprang apart, no linked
narratives, just *bam* then separate lives.

Foreign languages

‘When I don’t know a language, numbers are my handhold:
two fingers for baguettes, count the coins, remember
the street number, the keypad – we eat, we have shelter,
we have a bed for the night,’ says Y.

X snickers to himself. ‘I’m going to call you, *number 25*,’
he says, for the tingling pleasure of seeing Y’s face
fracture into uncertainty, then, ‘Oh oh oh,’ her complaining,
but it’s a foreign land so they have to whisper.

‘Protected by the secret of statistics’ – X flashes a card
featuring a wobbly translation at Y and S. ‘We’re undercover numbers –
our mission is to move the decimal point on tills forward.
There’ll be confusion throughout the land.’ He can tell
that Y at least, has perked up.

‘Gimme those lips,’ he grins at Y, enjoying the swagger
of the words. ‘You’re just copying that movie,’ she snips.
‘Those lips, those lips,’ he chants. His little black dog joins
as a yapping chorus. ‘Oh p-u-l-e-e-z-e,’ says S.

(Y is trying to break the stare between S and X, but the charged air
isn’t tissue or butter or anything she can count on.)

S wakes up

1.

'X is a bastard,' says the voice in the cave of S's brain,
where he's not officially thinking or saying anything (not
anything he'd admit), but where, in spite of the man
who wears the friendly face, a furious film sputters and jerks.

In the film, X is ahead, with many sales and invitations
to important conferences. 'X is resting his skinny arse
on past glory. His inventions have never been that good,'
says the voice. 'That last one, just faded ideas, tarted up.'

The film jumps to S himself in a field of withered swedes.
Around him, amongst the mute uncaring vegetables,
disintegrating boxes of his work. The earth is turned
from the sun. Years of S's life are in the frayed cardboard –
months spent laying out patterns over the living-room floor
until the moment of revelation, while X has a studio in town
with teenage assistants.

S wakes rubbing wetness from his cheeks – everything
he's poured his life into will amount to nothing. No!
In memory of his mother's blue eyes and narrow waist,
her only child will not be beaten. He'll make a show reel
about his work and send it to his connections (such
as they are) his heart and determination shining!

2.

X: ‘S’s brain is an overheated graphics card.’

Y:

X: ‘As soon as S’s connections see people returning
his flaky inventions, they’ll drop him.’

Y:

X: ‘Look, I don’t want to talk about S. I don’t want to think
about him. Why’d you keep bringing him up?’

Gifts

X buys Y a new car – just like the cramped
expensive brooches her father used to buy

her mother, thinks Y. What did her mother
think of the gifts? Did she see them as her husband

asserting his status in town (a businessman who could afford
rubies for his wife) or did she understand

the closely ornamented flowers as a kind of love?
What did her mother buy her father? Y can't remember

a single gift.

Reconstructions

Y is in her garden snapping at dead flower heads, fracturing plants into unknown languages. She recalls real-estate stickers ripped to 'So – old' and, from the bus, the thrill of watching 'urge' make 'Surgery'. Oh, she's in the mood for a big think – chickweed impulses, massive hydrangea questions –

> why is it hard to dive headfirst into older times?
>
> why hasn't she heard from R for months?
>
> is X really a mean person?
>
> does she spend all her time imagining others,
> and her feelings towards them, the way scientists
> construct lost animals from teeth or jaws?
>
> does she prefer the silent order of her mind
> with its chessboard emotions, to the bark of reality?
>
> is reality separate from her mind?

She could write a sonnet for X (or S or R), put a lid on her can of aloneness, but today she's busy grabbing at weeds and flicking her fork through warm soil.

THREE

On being unwilling to click 'I forgot my password'

For a while, living a digital life was like being
a successful swan. Dignified gliding over the lake
like you understood the way the world worked,
the world being hard bright stones at the bottom
of the lake and you on the surface, held up.

Then you forgot that word. There were hundreds
at your disposal: confetti, opera, ice cream, cat,
ekphrastic, blooming, blimming, dahlia –
you could dive into a roomful of tiny, crunchy
jigsaw pieces of words.

You know you're just holding onto the rope
out of cussedness. This involves sneaky excuses
that don't stack up and is not a quality
you admire in yourself, but keeps you holding on
like a mad terrier who's going to be exterminated
for believing that the grip of its little jaws
will drag the daylight through.

Or it's like refusing to jump
into the far below, feel the swoosh
of dark green closing over your head,
bubbles and squirming.

Or being the child crouched under the far
corner of the bed while the big ones
call and call.

A short history of sightseeing

Kia ora, admission includes: a grin and the right to finger
the history of wonders; a boy, crouched and anxious;

resolute men, hands in pockets, or boldly on the hip;
the hierarchies observed. The family desires

what they came for. The wonder of a waterfall!
The wonder of trout! Served after a stroll in genuine bush.

Imagine women in stifling skirts, crouched
inside a dwelling, a rumble from the mountain off stage.

Today, when the kids want out and the mind
darts towards egg sandwiches and slices

oozing caramel, it's world-class history –
when you step into the frame.

Instructed to write a poem called Home

Confused little teaspoon of thoughts, measured against
the picturesque void you claimed was the sky.
Roused from its battered wooden drawer, the teaspoon
rejected oceans and fire, but struggled for alternatives.
You suggested ferns or flax – though you could barely
identify them – an indigenous design or two, skin
from a sheep, et cetera; concentrated medicine
with a dash of bitterness to immunise against the flirty voices
of lifts. Yet, pedants insisted the potion originated *elsewhere* –
like pendants themselves with roots deep in the fertilised earth.
Undeterred, you squinted, lifted the mirror and called it 'At Home'.

Spring story

You have to listen to the stories
beans tell – rain pouring onto the earth,
the sun as a flasher, outrageous hair-
snatching, mouth-filling wind

translucent seed heads quivering
above rough dirt

the pursed mouths of young leaves,
cross as a man who's left his life
behind

us lumbering around like bears –
What must we eliminate?
Where are our chainsaws? –

and in the pot, steam rising
in maddened shapes, the beans begin
their voyage to flesh.

Touch phone

Daddy, you're a summer scratch on the windows
beside my bed. Touch: you're pictured on a lavender
thistle head – eight preposterous jointed legs, followed
by 10 top facts. You can't form a picture of me, but you use
two of the eight as white canes, tap tapping your way
around our house. Did you hatch in our elderly wallpaper,
its surface torn by the last cat, or under the gleaming
mataī floorboards we clomp around on? Touch: you hide
by gluing debris on your slender sac, and you've a talent
for pretending to be dead. Where did you go as I looked
to the sky, wondering what to wear in nor'west gales?
You can detach a leg and leave it twitching, your predators
baffled. Are you underfoot, under the windowsill's wide boards,
or headed for the mataī forest, where – touch – your mouth
could ingest our crumbs?

The silences

This morning I read that silence is good
for your brain. I'd followed the link
from Facebook to the anxious inside
of our bodies where we hurry around
trying to live longer. I remembered
the little grey mouse we chased
around the living room with our giant legs
and broom. How its tiny heart must
have nearly flown apart as it dashed
for the enormous sofa. What was it like
for the mouse in there? Googling mice,
I imagine the fragrance of old dust
and a blurry darkness.

*

The old man at the bus stop with his
stiff tweed cap and padded jacket

broke the bubble of my podcast
with announcements – the bus, late.

The road, not made when his kids
went to school. How lucky

we were to have clean water. How hard
they worked last century to get water

to the hill suburbs. Weak sunlight lay across
the tarry asphalt and angular houses

as I strained to catch the relieving rumble
of the bus.

*

This paper has no memory, the print rep –
a kindly man – said of the unsubdued
folds of my book, springing about like hair
on a bad day. It had no memory of the crack
of the fold, the silence between pines
as they waited for the chainsaw,
the smothering needles of the forest floor
silencing all other plants. And what of the mill
with its steel efficiency, the giving up of fibres
in union with others deemed white enough
in the long centuries into which paper is fed?

*

Forgetting is a kind of silence too
like trees that appear still

as we hurry past, but fed underground
by long roots, are growing imperceptibly.

Outside, a gaunt telephone pole
brings data to the iron-roofed cottages

below, where invisible people
work at their lives.

At Moeraki

Black curved swallows were everywhere
that late summer. Sleek fighter pilots
with no regard for cottages,
aerials or smart renovations,
they zoomed between roof and tree,
then out to sea and back again.
When black arrows whizzed through
the wide doors of our rented house,
it was like they'd darted through our bodies.
We felt the ocean flood the rooms.
The huge kitchen, with its green island
of steel sinks and impenetrable oven,
was no hiding place. What saved me was how
you cradled the lost fluttering ones
in your hands. On the deck, again and again,
you launched a shivering bird into the air.

*

One morning you instructed me
to put three birds in a poem.

'Look – evenly spaced,' you said.
I reluctantly admitted there were

three grey birds, evenly spaced,
on a black wire. 'A *haiku* perhaps,'

you grinned. Smartarse, I thought.
'And put in the mist!' Grey mist rolled

over the sky. For days afterwards,
I fretted about what I would put in.

*

Something in me believed that if we saw
the penguins, the missing harmony between us,
the birds and the ocean would be restored.
Seeing a penguin, in its solemn suit, would give us
our place of ease. One freezing afternoon
we drove to the cliff's edge. In the wooden hide,
carefully ignoring the other people, we lifted heavy
metal binoculars. One penguin stood high above
the steel sea. While seals flopped in and out
of the water and we pressed into the binoculars
until our eyes hurt, the stately bird shuffled
two steps up its cliff.

*

When I heard the scrabbling sound
and wheeled to see the little swallow
dancing in the woodstove's metal firebox,
all I could think was 'It looks like an astronaut.'
The squat swollen box with its stained glass
was the bird's helmet, and through it
we stared at each other.

*

You opened the firebox door and cupped
the agitated swallow until it escaped
and flew against the glass. We placed
the dazed bird outside on the wooden table.
For a long time it sat unmoving,
looking in at us. What did we look like –
two people in a rented house, pretending
they lived beside an ocean of grey brushstrokes?

All we could see was its dark bird eye.

Bees

1.

The bumblebees flew into our basement through the gap
under the old ginger-red door. From a bee perspective
they were heading for their nest. Some days, above the joists
and floorboards, music sounded – remote guitars, songs
like the daytime moon; sometimes *clonk, clonk, clonk.*
The bees crawled frantically across the earth, their precise
black legs crewing for the horizon. They disappeared
into jumbled darkness beyond folded garden chairs.
The pest man said bees didn't worry and made
their homes anywhere. He had three other bee jobs
that afternoon. He said, 'Stand back or they'll bite you,' though,
when I'd open the basement door, flooding their world
with brightness, the bees would fly towards my shape –
at the last moment, they'd swerve.

2.

oust   displace

                                            replace

3.

the balm of the definitions

4.

I remember a man (now dead), who told me if we abandoned
the city it'd be overtaken by pōhutukawa. The trees, with their
solemn leaves and 'Season's Greetings' crimson, would start

in cracks of buildings. A few years would pass, and then what –
a forest, a ruin? Ever since, I've noticed frazzled plants
breaking the asphalt; lichen staining the walls of buildings.
When I pull a weed from the gravel, I study the roots,
thin as cotton.

5.

Where can you put a rock so it looks normal?
The builders had levered up a pile – sharp and hard –
from under the earth. I staggered round the garden.
Beside the abundant hydrangeas? The raggedly
elegant renga rengas?

6.

make room for

                                        give place to

7.

The evening was a grey stillness. I'd been to the funeral
of a woman I knew and liked, who'd died suddenly.
High in the karo, tūī sang. I tipped my watering can
towards the impatiens struggling in terracotta pots.

Fall of the leaf

There's dryness that contains words like crunch and crack,
glamorous yellows baked to a shine, stained corpses, tissue
stretched between veins, former beauties faded to bone.
A woman whisking her broom across the asphalt tries
to articulate her feelings – like herding the world's variety
into a bag. The words anchor her to the leaves and path.
She doesn't want to sweep up every day – no matter how much
she likes the idea of water rushing down the red-tiled drain.

*

The woman buys a ring made from the F4 scrabble tile.
Fun and cheap, she thinks. She also knows her mind leapt
to fuck. To disguise this she tells her friends a list of words –
fine, free, fond, fern, fizz, flat, fail, fury – made her want
the ring. Her friends think of the camera aperture – one
that snaps the subject into focus, but leaves the rest
a blurred dream.

*

Every day new leaves fall – the slender point of olives, rounded
feet, scattered over the path. The woman wonders why.
One site tells her about autumn and how water can be stolen
by cold air. But this is summer, so she skips to heat, lack of water
or the puzzle of soil nutrition. Maybe the leaves are just old.
She stares at the screen. On the path, fine needles darken
from crimson to the purple-black of goth lipstick.

*

fire   fast   fans   fear   fame   flew   foil   flux

*

On TV there's news of gum trees burning – their elegant shapes
silhouetted in walls of flame. Her botanist neighbour
tells her about European settlers who, frightened by the dark
chaos of an unfamiliar forest and believing it limitless, cleared
the fastest way they knew, by burning. On the hills opposite
their houses the fire burned for three months, all the way
to the coast.

*

She stares at the hills that wrap the sky like the flank
of a large complicated animal. The hide is bright with new bush
and studded with houses from aspirational suburbs.
On bare ridges are the steely fairy tales of pylons.

*

The ring draws comments from a young waitress
with a liking for defiance. The woman thinks F4 must be
a litmus test. Leaves are scattered all over the path.
An essay she's reading asks whether 'daily life, ordinary life
is non-historical?' She looks to the ridges and the electric sky
above them, but wants to end with leaves, dried into the shape
of themselves, lying like surprises, anywhere they fall.

Notes

'New Zealand holiday': the line 'Moments/on either side falling like sheer cliffs' is adapted from a line in Teju Cole's essay 'Memories of Things Unseen', published in *Known and Strange Things* (Faber & Faber, 2016).

'Litter' is after Matthew Yeager's wonderful question poem 'A Jar of Balloons or the Uncooked Rice'.

'One life' refers to *An Intimate History of Humanity* (HarperCollins, 1994) by Theodore Zeldin.

The sequence of poems about X, Y, S and R were inspired by Nicole Krauss's *Great House* (WW Norton & Company, 2010) with its interlocking characters and their rich interior lives. X, Y, S and R are products of my imagination and wholly fictional.

'Spring story': the line 'you have to listen to the stories/ beans tell' is adapted from the Japanese film *Sweet Bean*, directed by Naomi Kawase.

Acknowledgements

Thanks to the journals, anthologies and competitions where many of these poems have appeared: *Sport*, *Landfall*, *Poetry New Zealand*, *The Spinoff*, *JAAM*, *Trout*, *Hue & Cry*, *Contrapasso*, *Bird Words*, *The Unexpected Greenness of Trees* and the Caselberg Trust 2019 International Poetry Prize.

The poems have had many friends and helpers along the way. Thank you to my wonderful writing group, the Meow Gurrrls: Mary-Jane Duffy, Abra Sandi King, Sudha Rao, Janis Freegard, Rewa Morgan, Kirsten Le Harivel and Mary Cresswell.

And further back my MA in Creative Writing classmates at the IIML: Gigi Fenster, Sue Orr, Lucy Orbell, Abby Stewart, Anna Taylor, Emma Gallagher, Kate Mahony, Craig Cliff and Tom Fitzsimmons.

To Greg O'Brien and Jenny Bornholdt, many thanks for reading the manuscript and for your input and caring. Thanks to Madison Hamill for the excellent editing suggestions, and to The Cuba Press for making it happen.

Most of all to Peter Black – for everything.

To see some of these poems live, visit the Meow Gurrrls YouTube channel.

marymacphoto.wordpress.com